PAINTING ON SUGAR

LESLEY HERBERT &
JEAN HODGKINSON

MEREHURST

To our mothers, Florence and Alice, for all
their help. With all our love, Lesley and Jean.

≈

Published in 1993 by Merehurst Limited, Ferry House,
51-57 Lacy Road, Putney, London SW15 1PR

Reprinted 1993

Copyright © Merehurst Limited 1993

ISBN 1 85391 196 8

Managing Editor Bridget Jones
Edited by Alison Leach
Designed by Jo Tapper
Photography by James Duncan
Colour separation by Fotographics Ltd, UK-Hong Kong
Printed by Craftprint Pte Limited, Singapore

The author and publisher would like to thank the following for their assistance:
Chocolate and Cakes, 79 Corbets Tey Road, Upminster, Essex
J.F. Renshaws Ltd., Mitcham House, River Court, Albert Drive, Woking, Surrey
GU21 5RP
Orchard Products, 49 Langdale Road, Hove, East Sussex BN3 4HR
Simon Elvin Ltd., Wooburn Industrial Park, Wooburn Green, Bucks HP10 OPE
Squires Kitchen, 3 Waverley Lane, Farnham, Surrey GU9 8BB
Twins Wedding Shop, 67/69 Victoria Road, Romford, Essex RM1 2LT

NOTES ON USING THE RECIPES
For all recipes, quantities are given in metric, Imperial and cup
measurements. Follow one set of measures only as they are not
interchangeable.
Standard 5ml teaspoons (tsp) and 15ml tablespoons (tbsp) are used.
Australian readers, whose tablespoons measure 20ml, should adjust
quantities accordingly. All spoon measures are assumed to be level
unless otherwise stated.
Eggs are a standard size 3 (medium) unless otherwise stated.

CONTENTS

INTRODUCTION

The art of painting on or with sugar provides a relaxing and enjoyable challenge. Many students who believe they cannot paint or draw are delighted with their first results in sugarwork. The answer is not to try and create images freehand but to trace existing, professional designs carefully . When painting, look for the light and dark shading or note whether figures have brown outlines. Gradually, as your confidence grows, you will be able to create individual images.

We start this book on the subject of cocoa painting which is one of the easiest methods as it uses only one colour but in different depths of light and shade. Once you have mastered this technique, move on to experimenting with dusting powders (blossom tints/petal dusts) in the same way. We were delighted with the effects achieved on royal icing, sugarpaste and runouts when we first attempted this technique. Instead of soaking into the royal icing or staining it as we feared, the combination of colours and fat produced a delicate, transparent appearance. So be adventurous and try this for yourself.

We have tried to include as many ideas for boys and men as possible, as this is not widely covered in other books. Remember that the motifs and skills used are often interchangeable, so if you do not have time for a long method, then substitute a quicker alternative. For example, instead of running out a car design you may prefer to paint it using the dusting powder and fat technique. If you feel like a challenge, you can try the decoupage technique for the same motif.

We hope you enjoy reading and using this book as much as we have enjoyed working together to produce the ideas and the text. Good luck!

Stencilled Christmas Cake, see page 55

Melt some cocoa butter or white vegetable fat (shortening) in a saucer over a bowl of hot water. Tilt the saucer to keep the fat to one side and add 1 tsp cocoa (unsweetened cocoa) away from the fat. Mix the fat and cocoa together gradually to obtain different depths of colour.

EXPERT ADVICE

≈

White vegetable fat (shortening) is cheaper than cocoa butter and a good substitute. Oil is not suitable as it does not set and the picture could be easily smudged.

~ 1 ~

CHRISTENING CAKE Using an HB pencil, trace the template, see page 64. Scribe the design onto the dry coated cake. Mix some cocoa with the chosen fat to a light cream colour to make a 'wash' for the background. Paint each section of the baby, avoiding the scribed lines.

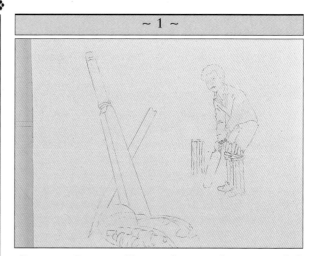

~ 1 ~

CRICKET DESIGN Trace the templates, see left and page 65, and transfer onto the cake. Take care not to use too much pressure when scribing as the lines would be hard to disguise.

~ 2 ~

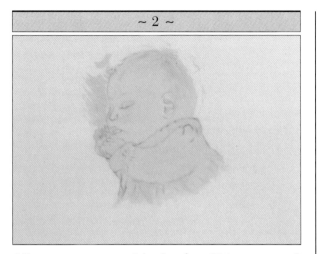

Mix more cocoa with the fat. Using a no. 3 paintbrush, paint in the medium shading. Then, using a no. 00 paintbrush, paint around the outline.

~ 3 ~

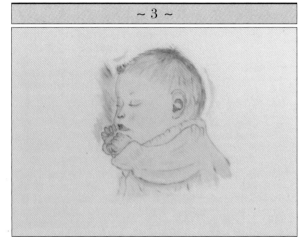

Reheat the water so that the fat is hot and can absorb more cocoa. Define the baby's features with a dark colour. Mix the fat and cocoa to a paste consistency for very dark areas.

~ 2 ~

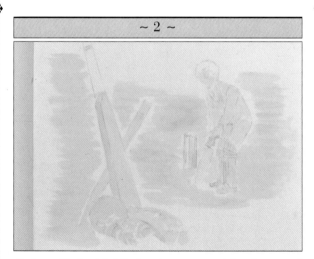

Paint all the highlighted areas and background with a weak solution of cocoa mixed with fat.

~ 3 ~

Paint all the shaded areas. Outline the motifs in a dark colour to emphasize them. A little black dusting powder (petal dust/blossom tint) can be added to the cocoa to give more depth to the hair and eyes.

CHRISTENING CAKE

20cm (8 in) round cake
apricot glaze
1kg (2 lb) marzipan (almond paste)
clear alcohol (gin or vodka)
1.25kg (2½ lb) sugarpaste
peach food colouring
small amount of peach royal icing
cocoa butter or white vegetable fat (shortening)

EQUIPMENT

28cm (11 in) round cake board
no. 0/4, 00 and 3 sable paintbrushes
greaseproof paper (parchment)
HB pencil
scriber
no. 0 and 1 piping tubes (tips)
wax paper
1m (1 yd 3 in) picot ribbon to trim cake and
board edge

● Brush the cake with apricot glaze and cover with marzipan (almond paste). Allow to dry for a couple of days. Colour the sugarpaste peach. Brush the marzipan with clear alcohol. Coat the cake and board separately with the peach sugarpaste. Leave to dry for several days.

● Using a no. 0 piping tube (tip) and royal icing, pipe eight lace booties, see templates page 64, onto wax paper and leave to dry.

● Cut out two circles of greaseproof paper (parchment): one 20cm (8 in), the other 28cm (11 in). Trace the template of the baby, see page 64, in the centre of the smaller circle. Fold both circles into eight and cut a scalloped edge to produce an eight-petalled shape. Place the larger circle on the board and scribe around the outline. Attach the cake to the board with a small bulb of royal icing.

● Scribe around the template of the smaller circle on the top of the cake, taking care that the scallops are in line with the ones on the board.

● Trace the baby's picture on the cake. Paint the baby in cocoa following the step-by-step instructions, see pages 6 – 7.

● Attach ribbon around the bottom edge of the cake and around the board. Pipe a small shell border around the base of the cake with a no. 0 piping tube (tip) and peach royal icing. Pipe embroidery, see template page 64, around the scallops on the cake and board, using the same tube (tip) and icing.

● Using a no. 1 piping tube (tip), pipe eight bows, 2.5cm (1 in) from the top of the cake on the side and attach the lace booties. Pipe the lines from the bow to each bootie. An inscription can be added if required.

EXPERT ADVICE

≈

Mistakes can be rectified by cleaning the brush in melted fat and brushing over the errors. Continue cleaning the brush and lifting off the cocoa until it is completely removed. Do not work on this area until dry.

Take some close-up photographs of friends' babies in profile. Trace the details and enlarge the tracing on a photocopier to give a good supply of baby motifs.

PAINTING WITH DUSTING POWDER

$\mathcal{F}$ollow the steps, right, for creating a painting medium by combining dusting powders (petal dusts/blossom tints) with fat.

EQUIPMENT
greaseproof paper (parchment)
HB pencil
scriber
cocoa butter or white vegetable fat (shortening)
knife
selection of dusting powders (petal dusts/blossom tints)
paintbrushes
absorbent kitchen paper
clean-up tool (used by potters, available in art shops)

As for cocoa painting, white vegetable fat (shortening) is cheaper than cocoa butter. Oil is not suitable. This method of combining dusting powders with melted fat provides a versatile medium for multi-coloured designs. It is an excellent way of extending your skills when you have mastered the basic principles of cocoa painting.

EXPERT ADVICE

≈

Melt a little cocoa butter or white vegetable fat to clean the brushes. When changing colours, do not use water as oil and water do not mix and the brush becomes hard. To clean brushes after use, wash thoroughly in soapy water.

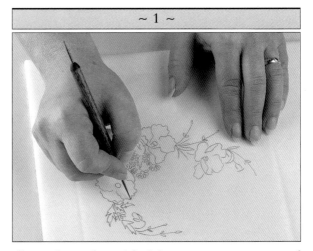

~ 1 ~

Coat the cake with icing or sugarpaste and allow to dry for about 3 days. Trace the design on greaseproof paper (parchment). Using a scriber, transfer it onto the cake through the paper. When the paper is removed, a thin scratch line can be seen.

~ 4 ~

Do not have too much colour on the brush. Wipe the brush on a piece of absorbent kitchen paper to remove the excess colour. Paint fine lines, such as hair or fur from the root outwards; remember to brush in the direction of hair growth.

~ 2 ~

Put the cocoa butter or white vegetable fat (shortening) in the centre of a plate over a pan or bowl of boiling water. Use a knife tip to put the dusting powders (petal dusts/blossom tints) around the plate edge; the fat will melt quickly making it easy to mix with the colourings.

~ 3 ~

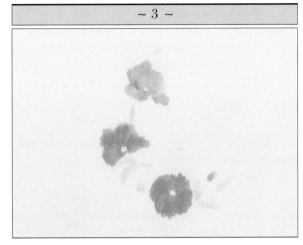

Mix the dusting powder with the fat to the required colour strength and begin by painting the lightest colour in the flowers and leaves. Clean the paintbrushes in the cup of melted fat before changing colours.

~ 5 ~

If the fat is kept hot, you will be able to mix in more dusting powder to obtain deep rich colours. Use a brush with a tip which forms a point when wet. The brush should not be too soft but should spring back into shape when painting.

~ 6 ~

Texture can be added by scratching some of the colour away with a pin or sharp tool. If you make a mistake, allow the fat to set, then with the clean-up tool or scalpel, scrape the colour from the edge into the centre. Enough colour will be removed to enable you to start again.

HARVEST CAKE

18cm (7 in) square rich fruit cake
apricot glaze
1kg (2 lb) marzipan (almond paste)
clear alcohol (gin or vodka)
1.25kg (2½ lb) sugarpaste
small amount of flower paste
small amount of royal icing
cocoa butter or white vegetable fat (shortening)
selection of dusting powders (petal
dusts/blossom tints)
20 sugar daisies
32 pieces grass

EQUIPMENT

25cm (10 in) square cake board
1.5m (1⅔ yd) x 3mm (⅛ in) ribbon
scalpel
scissors
no. 2 piping tube (tip)
sable paintbrushes

● Before cutting the corners off the square cake, mark the surface with a glass or round cutter to ensure an even shape. Brush the cake with apricot glaze and cover with marzipan (almond paste). Allow to dry for a couple of days. Brush the marzipan with clear alcohol and coat with white sugarpaste. Leave to dry for several days.

● Make a pattern for the ribbon insertion. Measure the top and sides of the coated cake and cut a piece of greaseproof paper (parchment) which is large enough to cover the top of the cake and extend down to the base on all sides. Mark the position of the top edge on the paper, then cut away the corner pieces so that the pattern fits over the cake neatly.

● Trace the template, see page 65, in the centre of the greaseproof pattern. Take care that all pencil lines are on the outside of the pattern so that they do not mark the sugarpaste coating. Lay the pattern on the cake and pin it in position. Scribe the design through the paper.

● Cut short pieces of ribbon. Use a sharp scalpel to make small cuts in the sugarpaste coating and insert the ends of a piece of ribbon into each one.

● Use a no. 2 piping tube (tip) and white royal icing to pipe a small shell border around the base of the cake. Following the step-by-step instructions on pages 10 – 11, paint the poppy design. Place a small ball of sugarpaste on each corner and cover with sprays of daisies and grass to conceal the balls of paste.

EXPERT ADVICE

≈

Apricot glaze is made by boiling and sieving apricot jam. The glaze should be boiled before it is applied to the cake so that it will keep well.

BASIC TECHNIQUE FOR BRUSH EMBROIDERY

*B*rush embroidery is an easy and effective way of decorating cakes or plaques. It is often used for flower motifs, but can also be used in other ways, such as for the folds in a dress or bride's veil. When combined with other techniques such as painting or runouts, brush embroidery helps to give an added dimension to your work.

EQUIPMENT
no. 0, 1 and 2 piping tubes (tips)
greaseproof paper (parchment)
scriber
no. 1, 5 and 8 paintbrushes
clear piping gel
royal icing
selection of food colourings

Follow the steps, right, as a basic guide to the brush embroidery technique. When you are familiar with the method, try applying it to your own designs.

~ 1 ~

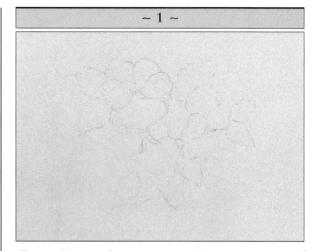

Trace the template, see page 71, on greaseproof paper (parchment). Scribe the design onto the cake through the paper. Add 1 tsp clear piping gel to a cup of full-peak royal icing. The piping gel will slow down the speed at which the icing sets.

~ 4 ~

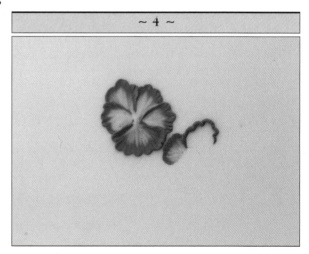

Large flowers or petals are easier to work on than smaller shapes. Outline the petal which appears furthest away with a no. 2 piping tube (tip); do not outline more than one petal at a time. Apply more pressure to the piping bag as you work towards the centre of the petal.

~ 2 ~

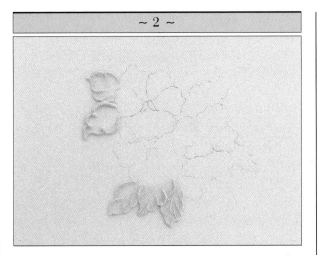

Outline the leaves with green royal icing and a no. 1 piping tube (tip). Pipe dots of the icing on the inside edge of the leaf points on the larger leaves.

~ 3 ~

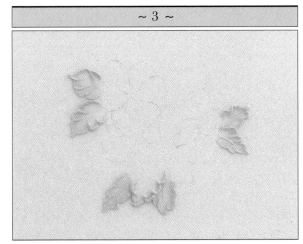

Using a damp paintbrush, smooth the icing towards the centre vein of the leaf. The aim is to soften the outline and not to brush the icing all over the leaf. The dots of icing will help to give a veined appearance. Pipe a line down the centre of the leaf to complete the effect.

~ 5 ~

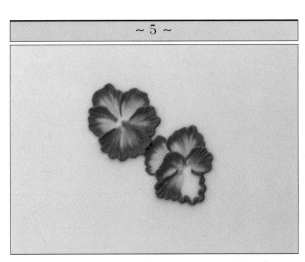

Brush the icing towards the centre of the flower with a damp brush, leaving the icing thicker on the outside edge of the petal. An attractive effect is obtained by also leaving the icing thicker where the petals overlap.

~ 6 ~

Complete the flower when the icing is dry; paint stems and any details with food colourings. Use a no. 0 piping tube (tip) to pipe small dots to represent stamens.

NANNA CAKE

25 x 20cm (10 x 8 in) oval cake
apricot glaze
1.25kg (2½ lb) marzipan (almond paste)
clear alcohol (gin or vodka)
1.75kg (3½ lb) sugarpaste
250g (8 oz) royal icing
clear piping gel
selection of food colourings

E Q U I P M E N T

33 x 28cm (13 x 11 in) oval board
1.5m (1⅔ yd) x 5mm (¼ in) each of pink, lilac
and lemon ribbon
1.5m (1⅔ yd) x 5mm (¼in) ribbon to trim
board
no. 1, 2 and 4 piping tubes (tips)
no. 0, 0/4 and 3 paintbrushes

● Brush the cake with apricot glaze and cover it with marzipan (almond paste). Allow to dry for a couple of days. Brush the marzipan with clear alcohol and coat with sugarpaste. Coat the board separately with sugarpaste. Allow to dry for several days. Attach the cake to the board with a bulb of royal icing.

● Trace the templates of the pansies and butterfly, see page 67 and right, and scribe the design on the top and front side of the cake. Brush embroider the flowers and leaves following the step-by-step instructions, see pages 14 and 15, using the no. 2 tube. Remember to begin with the leaf or petal which appears furthest away as this will give another dimension to your work.

● Mark a line around the side of the cakes leaving a space for the flowers at the front. Attach the pink ribbon with dots of royal icing. Attach the lemon and lilac ribbon above and below the pink ribbon, taking care to keep the spaces equal and the ribbons straight. Trim the ends of the ribbons on a slant. Tie two bows in each coloured ribbon and attach to the cake with royal icing.

● Using a no. 4 piping tube (tip) and white royal icing, pipe bulbs of icing around the base of the cake, leaving a small space between each bulb. Overpipe the border with loops of green royal icing using a no. 1 piping tube (tip).

● Scribe the inscription on the cake and pipe with a no. 1 tube (tip) and royal icing. Brush embroider the butterfly wings, using the same method as for the flower petals. When the icing is dry, paint the details in pink food colouring and pipe the body of the butterfly.

See also violets template, page 67

BRUSH EMBROIDERY VARIATIONS

*T*hese steps illustrate two methods of varying the basic brush embroidery technique. The first method is very useful if the flower has a pale outer edge and a deeper colour in the centre. Try these different techniques of colouring brush embroidery to obtain attractive and realistic effects.

Double outline method

See page 65 for painting method template

~ 1 ~

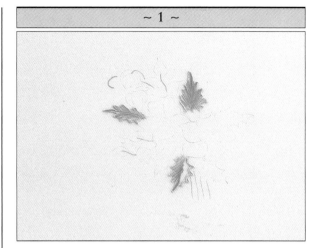

PAINTING METHOD *Scribe the design on the cake or plaque. Dilute a few drops of a food colouring that will contrast with the colour of icing being used. Outline the petal; the piping tube (tip) size will depend on the size of the flower – a no. 1 piping tube (tip) was used here.*

~ 1 ~

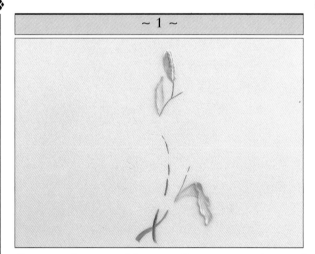

DOUBLE OUTLINE METHOD *Prepare two bags of icing either of different colours or a light and dark tint of the same colour. Prepare the design on the cake and outline the petal which appears furthest away.*

~ 2 ~

Dip the brush in the colouring, removing the excess on absorbent kitchen paper and leaving the brush damp. Brush the icing towards the centre of the leaf or petal.

~ 3 ~

Rinse the brush often to remove any icing. If the brush becomes sticky, it is difficult to achieve a neat smooth appearance.

~ 2 ~

Change to the other piping bag and pipe another row of icing against the outline. Use a damp brush to smooth the two icings together.

~ 3 ~

Continue outlining each petal or leaf in turn. It is important to rinse the brush frequently in clean water.

FAN CAKE

15cm (6 in) fan-shaped cake
apricot glaze
750g (1½ lb) marzipan (almond paste)
clear alcohol (gin or vodka)
1kg (2 lb) sugarpaste
small amount of royal icing
small amount of white flower paste or
pastillage
clear piping gel
selection of food colourings
70 cut-out blossom flowers
E Q U I P M E N T
23cm (9 in) fan-shaped board
fan-shaped button
no. 1 and 2 piping tubes (tips)
selection of paintbrushes
1m (1 yd 3in) x 5mm (¼ in) pink ribbon

● Brush the cake with apricot glaze and cover with marzipan (almond paste). Allow to dry for a couple of days. Brush the marzipan with clear alcohol and coat with sugarpaste. Whilst the icing is still soft, emboss the sugarpaste with the little fan shapes (using a button). Coat the board separately with sugarpaste. Leave the cake and board to dry.

● Attach the cake to the board with a small bulb of royal icing. Pipe a small shell border round the cake base, using yellow royal icing and a no. 1 piping tube (tip).

● Trace the template of the geisha girl, right, and scribe on the top of the cake. Paint her face, arms and shoes, using the method on pages 10 –11. Her hair and robe are brush-embroidered. Starting at the area which appears furthest away, brush the icing in the direction the fabric would fold naturally. Pipe a flower

for her hair or use a cut-out flower.

● Cut out the fan, right, from white flower paste or pastillage. Leave to dry; then paint the background and pipe some small dot flowers to form a pattern. Attach to the figure with a small bulb of icing.

● Attach cut-out flowers to the top edge of the cake, about 3cm (1½ in) apart. Using a no. 1 piping tube (tip) and white royal icing, pipe three little circles and some shells to resemble leaves to make an effective embroidered border. Attach groups of three blossoms with royal icing to the side of the cake between each fan shape. Pipe tiny leaves or shells on each flower.

● Complete the cake by attaching the ribbon to the board; double-sided sticky tape is very useful for this.

STRAWBERRY GATEAU

*T*his design looks beautiful on a celebration cake for anyone keen on gardening, ideal for Father's Day, but do put an inscription to make it personal and special.

20cm (8 in) round cake (genoese or madeira)
125g (4 oz/⅓ cup) strawberry jam
250g (8 oz) buttercream
apricot glaze
750g (1½ lb) sugarpaste or marzipan (almond paste)
cream food colouring
small amount of royal icing
5 large cut-out white blossom flowers with yellow piped centres

EQUIPMENT

25cm (10 in) round cake board
Fimo modelling clay (available from art and hobby shops)
no. 1 and 4 piping tubes (tips)
selection of paintbrushes

● Cut the cake into three 1cm (½ in) thick slices. Sandwich together with strawberry jam and buttercream. Coat the outside with a thin layer of buttercream. Place in refrigerator until firm but not frozen.

● Colour the sugarpaste, if using, with cream food colouring. Brush the cake with apricot glaze and cover with marzipan (almond paste) or cream coloured, flavoured sugarpaste. Leave overnight for the coating to become firm.

● To make a strawberry mould, knead the Fimo modelling clay until soft. Press half an underripe fresh strawberry gently into the clay, then remove the fruit. If you are pleased with the impression, bake the clay as directed by the manufacturer. Leave the mould until it is cold before using it. Press a piece of white marzipan into the mould, then remove and cut off excess marzipan, leaving half a white strawberry. Airbrush or dust with red and green dusting powders (petal dusts/blossom tints) to get a realistic effect.

● Trace the template of the strawberry design, see pages 66 and 71, and scribe only the leaves and stems on the gâteau top and sides. Brush embroider the leaves, using the method on pages 14 – 15. Brushing the icing with diluted food colouring gives an interesting effect. Use small bulbs of royal icing to attach the strawberries and flowers.

VARIATIONS

● Other seasonal fruits may be moulded in the same way as strawberries, particularly berry fruits, such as blackberries and raspberries.

● Brush embroider the background leaves as for the main cake. Instead of moulding the fruit, select perfect examples of fresh fruit and add them to the cake at the last minute.

The steps here show how the motor bike design is created; however, the same basic technique can be used for a wide variety of other designs.

When creating simple shapes, the design may be cut out after it is traced on the rice paper. Since the gel does not set but remains sticky, it is easier to handle the cutting out at this stage. However, rice paper has a tendency to curl up and any fine shapes, for example with pointed areas, are better left as outlines on the sheet until the gel painting is complete, then cut out at the end, see step 6.

EXPERT ADVICE

≈

Rice paper is available in a variety of different colours and thicknesses from cake decorating suppliers.

~ 1 ~

Place a sheet of rice paper over the design, see page 68, with the shiny side down, trace the design onto the rice paper using a black food colouring pen. Cut out the picture at this stage or at the end, see left.

~ 4 ~

If there are any lumps in the piping gel, use a palette knife to 'butter' or rub them smooth. Paint the helmet and visor.

~ 2 ~

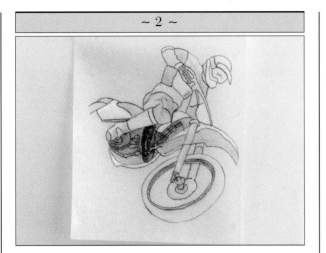

Mix some clear piping gel with the required food colourings on a small palette to a suitable depth of colour. Royal icing may be added to the piping gel to produce white or tints of colours. Using a no. 2 or 3 paintbrush, paint in all the light areas.

~ 3 ~

Place a small amount of paste food colourings on a small white tile or plate. Dip the brush into the piping gel and mix with the chosen colour to obtain a strong colour. Shade in the deeper areas over the parts previously painted.

~ 5 ~

Paint in all the black areas, and adjust any darker shading. When changing colours, wash the brush in water and dry on absorbent kitchen paper before applying the brush to the piping gel again. If the rice paper gets wet, it will begin to dissolve.

~ 6 ~

Draw the wheel spokes free-hand using a food colouring pen. Paint the ground using green, yellow and brown piping gel. If required, the design can now be cut out but remember the piping gel remains sticky. Attach the design to the cake with royal icing or piping gel.

RACING BIKE

18cm (7 in) square cake
apricot glaze
750g (1½ lb) marzipan (almond paste)
clear alcohol (gin or vodka)
1kg (2 lb) sugarpaste
250g (8 oz) royal icing
clear piping gel
selection of paste food colourings
rice or wafer paper
black food colouring pen
EQUIPMENT
25cm (10 in) square cake board
elastic band
no. 1 crimper
scissors
rice paper
tile or plate
selection of sable paintbrushes
no. 42 and 44 piping tubes (tips)
1.25m (1⅓ yd) navy blue ribbon
1.25m (1⅓ yd) x 1cm (½ in) silver paper
band for cake board edge

● Place the fruit cake on a sheet of greaseproof paper (parchment). Brush the cake with apricot glaze and cover with marzipan. Allow to dry. Brush clear alcohol over the marzipan and cover with sugarpaste.

● Place an elastic band around the ends of the crimper to keep them firmly closed. Press the crimper into the sugarpaste coating, making a design around the top border. Leave to dry.

● Using a piece of rice paper large enough to cover the template, see page 68, trace the design. Complete the work on the racing bike design, following the instructions on pages 24 and 25.

● Place the cake on a cake board. Pipe shells around the base of the cake with a no. 44 piping tube (tip) and white royal icing. Overpipe the shells with 'S' scrolls using a no. 42 piping tube (tip). Attach the ribbon around the side of the cake and secure the ends with dots of icing, taking care the join is at the back. Tie a bow with the excess ribbon and attach to the front of the cake. Trim the edge of the cake board with silver paper band.

EXPERT ADVICE
≈

This design is popular with young boys and the gel-painting technique is ideal for the design. However, if preferred, the gel may be piped into the different areas of the picture to create a runout effect. Trace the bike onto the rice paper with the black food colouring pen, then runout the shapes with gel, working directly on the cake.

SILHOUETTES

*S*ilhouette painting, or shadow painting as it is sometimes called, is a very old art form. There are dated silhouettes in the paleolithic caves. It is thought that shadows of people or animals were outlined on the walls and then coloured. A similar art form is shadow puppetry, or Chinese cut paper work. It is one of the simplest methods of obtaining a recognizable figure without having to worry about painting features.

The possibilities of using silhouettes in cake decorating are becoming recognized. The technique has been somewhat overlooked – or maybe taken for granted as it is so simple – but the effects can be stunning.

Here are some ideas you can try.

● Find a picture of a girl's profile. Trace it onto a small white plaque, paint the background only in blue, using the method opposite. Such cameo pictures can personalize the sides or top of a cake.

● Look in brochures or magazines for pictures of boats, cars or aeroplanes. Sometimes these can be difficult to paint in detail but they make effective silhouettes, especially for men's cakes for which students find it difficult to think of designs.

● Christmas trees, choir boys, Father Christmas, pets and wild animals are always effective. Babies, children, dancers, sports people ... the possibilities are endless. If at first you find drawing your own designs too difficult, there are many books on this subject available for artists, in which a vast selection of designs is already done for you.

● If you find painting in black unappetizing, try painting in dark brown on a cream cake or plaque, or wedgwood blue or green.

Templates for Anniversary Cake, page 30

Happy Anniversary

┌─────────────────────────────────┐

EXPERT ADVICE

≈

Using dusting powder (petal dust/blossom tint) and egg white is preferable; using a paste food colouring will give the same effect but will take a very long time to dry.

└─────────────────────────────────┘

~ 1 ~

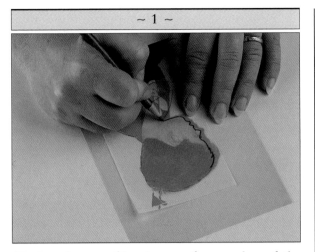

Find a clear profile picture of a member of the family, pet or pictures from books or magazines. Trace the profile very carefully. The picture may need to be reduced or enlarged on a photocopier. Scribe through the tracing onto the cake or plaque.

~ 2 ~

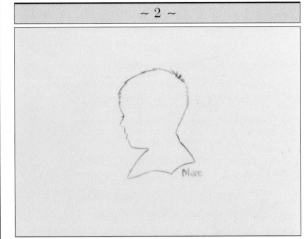

Mix black dusting powder (petal dust/blossom tint) with egg white to make a deep black paint. Using a fine brush, paint the outline of the silhouette. It is important to keep to the scribe line on a face; any slight errors will prevent the silhouette from being recognized.

~ 3 ~

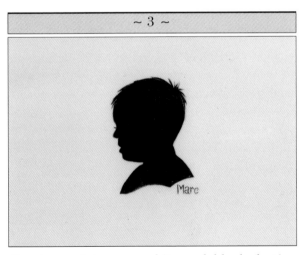

Continue mixing egg white and black dusting powder to the palette. If the mixture dries, just add extra egg white. Paint in the silhouette using a no. 5 paintbrush. Try to brush in one direction. If the silhouette is not dark enough, add extra black dusting powder to the mixture.

~ 4 ~

Silhouettes are a quick but personal and effective way to decorate cakes. The design of a couple dancing in the tradition of Fred Astaire would be ideal for an engagement or anniversary cake.

ANNIVERSARY CAKE

25cm (10 in) round cake
apricot glaze
1.25kg (2½ lb) marzipan (almond paste)
1.25kg (2½ lb) royal icing
pink and gold food colouring
black dusting powder (petal dust/blossom tint)
EQUIPMENT
33cm (13 in) round cake board
greaseproof paper (parchment)
airbrush • wax paper
no. 0, 1 and 2 piping tubes (tips)
1.25m (1⅓ yd) pink and gold ribbon to trim
board

● Brush the cake with apricot glaze and cover with marzipan (almond paste). Coat with royal icing. Coat the cake board with royal icing separately. When the icing is completely dry, remove any blemishes and the mark from the side scraper with a small, sharp knife.

● Cut out an 18cm (7 in) circle of cardboard and a strip of paper of the same depth and circumference as the cake. Fold the paper into six equal pieces and cut the scallop, below. Wrap the paper around the upper portion of the cake side and lay the cardboard circle on the top of the cake.

● Airbrush the exposed top and side of the cake with pink food colouring. Alternatively, use a wide brush and pink dusting powder, taking care always to brush away from the paper and cardboard to prevent the colour from spreading under the template and spoiling the effect. Attach the cake to the prepared board with a small bulb of royal icing.

● Pipe 75 lace pieces onto wax paper, using a no. 0 piping tube (tip). Leave to dry. Trace the templates of the figures and inscription, see page 28, and scribe onto the cake, following the step-by-step instructions on page 29.

● Pipe loops over the scallop line on the side using a no. 2 piping tube (tip) and royal icing. Tilt the cake towards you and pipe small loops from the first piped line with a no. 1 piping tube (tip) to give a lacy effect. Pipe a row of bulbs using a no. 2 piping tube (tip) around the base of the cake, taking care to avoid any peaks on the bulbs. Using a no. 1 piping tube (tip), pipe smaller bulbs to form a picot border.

● Pipe the inscription and bows on the side of the cake. When the icing is dry, paint these with gold food colouring. Remove the lace pieces from the wax paper, attach first to the edge of the inner circle on the cake top, then to the edge of the cake. Trim the cake board with pink and gold ribbon.

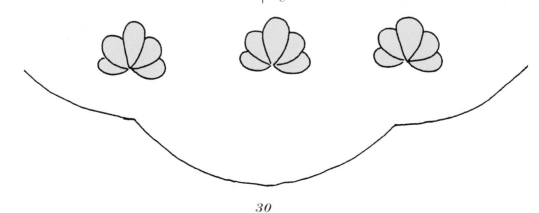

~ 1 ~

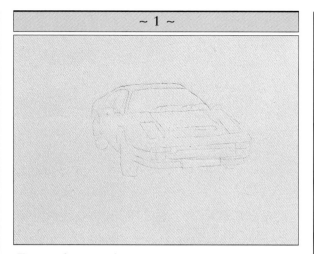

Trace the template, see page 34, and scribe through the paper onto the key. Put some food colourings on a palette and use water or clear alcohol to dilute the colours.

~ 2 ~

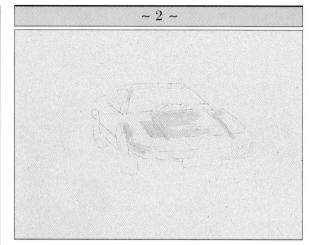

Taking care not to allow the brush to be too wet, paint the highlighted areas of the car body using a very pale colour. Keep wiping any excess moisture from the brush onto absorbent kitchen paper, otherwise the pastillage will become grainy.

~ 4 ~

Paint the body of the car with a no. 2 brush, avoiding highlighted areas and shading where necessary. Use a fine brush and a dark colour to paint grid lines on the wings and bonnet. Paint the wheels and front grid light grey and the headlights and indicator light tangerine.

~ 5 ~

Using a fine brush, paint all the black areas and outline all the traced lines in black. Paint four vertical lines on the tyres with a zig-zag pattern in between each line to represent the tread.

~ 3 ~

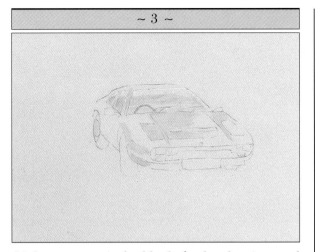

Make a grey wash: black food colouring and plenty of water or alcohol. Dry the brush and paint upholstery (follow staggered lines) inside windscreen. Paint steering wheel. Using fine paintbrush and blue wash, paint diagonal lines on windows, windscreen and headlights.

~ 6 ~

If the car design is not being added to a key and you just want a motif to keep, only cut out just the car silhouette from pastillage, leave to dry and paint as previously described.

SILHOUETTE KEY

23 x 15cm (9 x 6 in) oblong fruit cake
1kg (2 lb) marzipan (almond paste)
1.5kg (3 lb) sugarpaste
small amount of pastillage
125g (4 oz) royal icing
selection of food colourings
cornflour (cornstarch)

EQUIPMENT

23 x 15cm (9 x 6 in) thin cake board
30 x 23cm (12 x 9 in) oblong cake board
greaseproof paper (parchment)
HB pencil • ruler
scalpel • oil board (manilla board)
airbrush
no. 0, 1 and 42 piping tubes (tips)
scriber
no. 0/4 and 2 paintbrushes (good quality)
1.25 m (1⅓ yd) ribbon to trim cake board
masking tape • gold lustre colour

● Place the cake on the thin cake board. Cover with marzipan and leave to dry, then cover with two-thirds of the sugarpaste. Coat the cake board with the remaining sugarpaste.

● Trace the key template, see page 34, and cut it out in pale cream pastillage. Leave to dry.

● Cut a piece of oil board the depth and width of the longest sides of the cake. Trace the diamond and cross designs, see page 34, onto separate pieces of greaseproof paper (parchment). Before transferring the design to the oil board, decide on the position of the design. Rule a line on the oil board and trace on the diamond shape. Cut out carefully with a scalpel and ruler. Follow the same procedure on another board and cut out the cross design.

continued on page 34

continued from page 33

● Place the cake on a large piece of greaseproof paper to protect the work surface and surrounding area. Airbrush the design following step-by-step instructions, see pages 48 – 49. Attach the cake to the board with a small bulb of royal icing. Pipe a shell border using a no. 42 piping tube (tip) and royal icing.

● Smooth any rough areas on the pastillage key. Trace the car onto the key. Paint the car following the step-by-step instructions, see pages 32 – 33. Dust the rest of the key with gold lustre colour. Using a no. 2 piping tube (tip), pipe a line in tangerine royal icing along the key. Then pipe a line in brown royal icing along the side, using a no.1 piping tube (tip). Using the same colours and piping tubes (tips), pipe graduated lines around the head of the key.

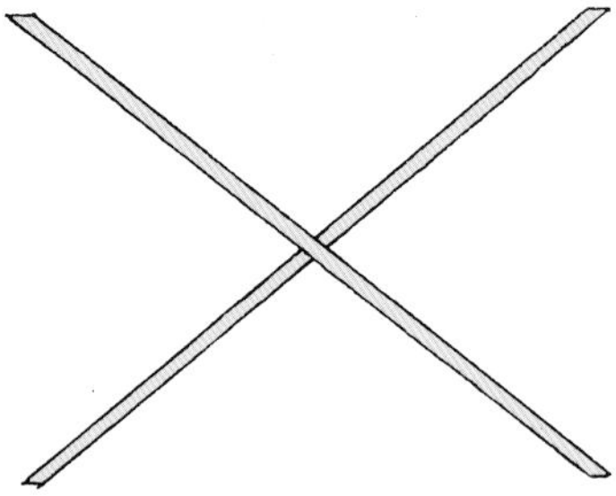

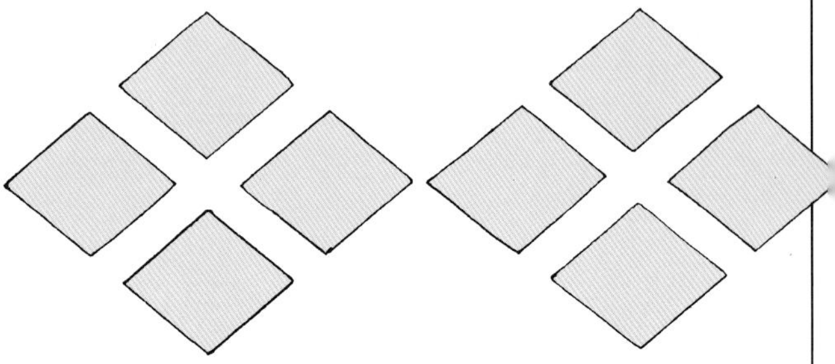

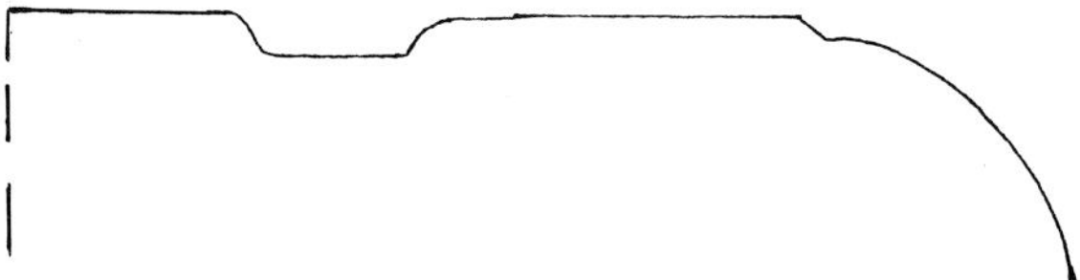

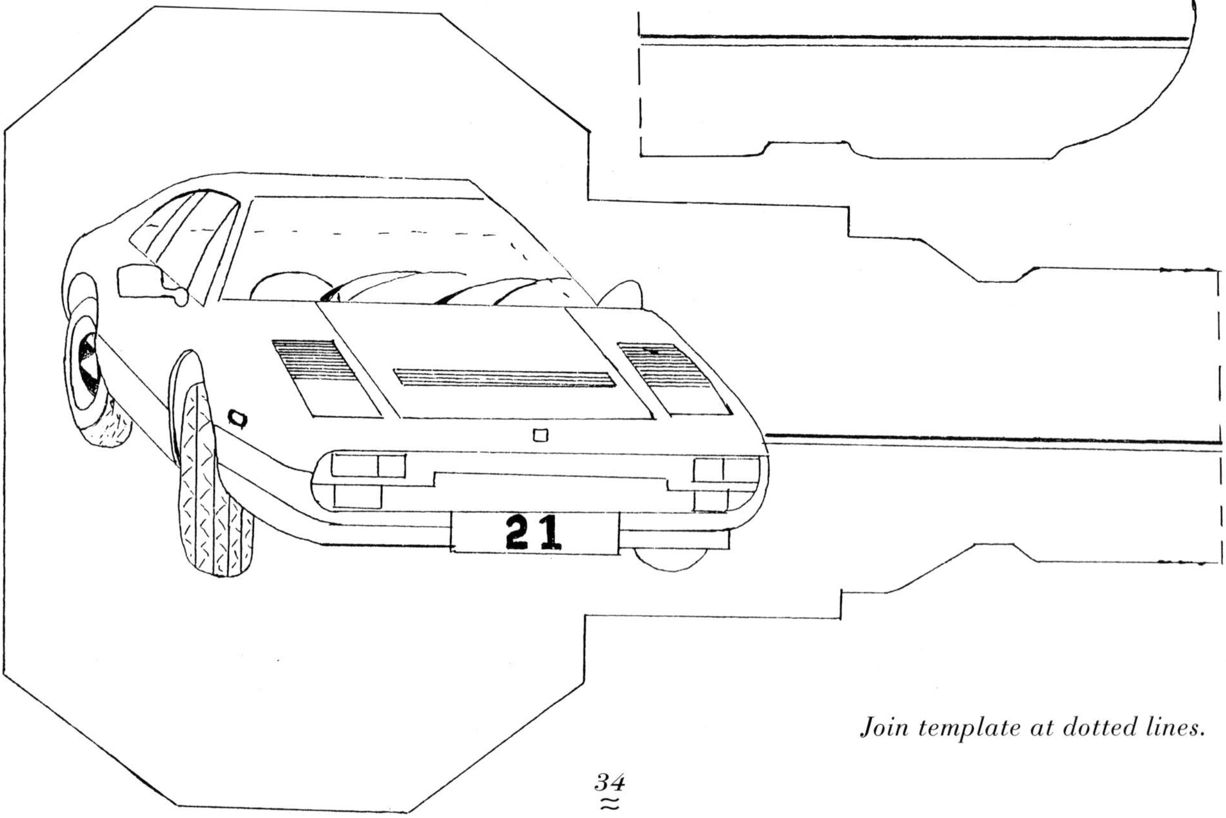

Join template at dotted lines.

34

DIRECT PAINTING

*P*ainting on sugar with food colourings is a very relaxing, enjoyable way to decorate a cake. It is easier to begin by painting on sugarpaste as this is not very absorbent and the surface of the coating does not dissolve too quickly.

Always allow the sugarpaste coating to dry for at least a week before painting it. In this time the surface will become firm and the risk of marking the coating with your fingers or hand when painting will be reduced.

If painting on a cake coated with royal icing, it is important to observe the following points. The final coat of icing should be reduced in consistency. If a knife is drawn through the bowl of icing, the mark should disappear in 15 – 20 seconds. Dry the icing quickly under a warm lamp (not too hot or the oil in the marzipan (almond paste) may stain the coating). A smooth, shiny coating is less absorbent than a matt grained surface, which will draw the colour and make the finish resemble blotting paper.

BASIC TECHNIQUE

Trace the design on a piece of greaseproof paper using an HB pencil. Carefully draw over the details on the reverse side of the paper. Place the template on the cake and first scribe the outline, then, taking care not to move the paper, all the details.

Place a selection of liquid or paste food colourings on a plate. If the colours are strong, dilute them with water or clear alcohol. For flesh colouring, put a few drops of water on the plate, dip the tip of the brush in paprika and mix it with the water; it should be very pale.

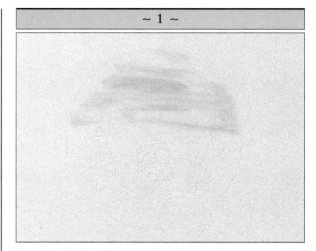

~ 1 ~

Paint the background colours first. Keep the brush almost dry, removing excess moisture on absorbent kitchen paper. If the brush is too wet or if you work on one area for too long, the surface will begin to dissolve, spoiling the surface.

~ 4 ~

Having a coloured picture as a guide is a considerable help. Paint areas of colour in the lightest tints. Following the picture, apply more colour to the shaded areas. Some pictures are best outlined in brown; this will help to lift the design and make it appear bold.

~ 2 ~

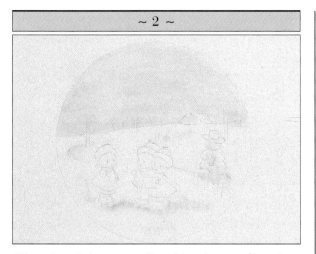

Rinse brush in water. Brushing in one direction, blend background colours. Dusting powder can also be used for background effects. Use large brush to apply and blend colours with icing (confectioners') sugar (not recommended if surface has slight cracks or is rough).

~ 3 ~

Paint the trees. Make small downward-slanting strokes and use a selection of green and blue colours, blending the colours together gradually.

~ 5 ~

Gradually paint the shading and details on the figures. Caricatures are often easier to paint and they can look effective. Remember to paint hair or fur from the root in the direction of growth. Do not add deep colours too quickly – you can always paint a deeper shade on top.

~ 6 ~

Lace, ribbon insertion, embroidery or crimping are all ideal techniques to use for framing the picture. Painting white on a white background can be difficult, but if you use light blue to shadow areas such as snow scenes, you will be able to create more depth.

CHRISTMAS CAKE

small trifoil cake
apricot glaze
1kg (2 lb) marzipan (almond paste)
clear alcohol (gin or vodka)
1.5kg (3 lb) sugarpaste
small amount of royal icing
small amount of flower paste or pastillage
selection of food colourings
EQUIPMENT
28cm (11 in) round cake board
greaseproof paper (parchment)
HB pencil
scriber
no. 0/4, 1 and 5 sable paintbrushes
no. 0 and 2 piping tubes (tips)
tree cutter ● wax paper

● Brush the cake with apricot glaze and cover it with marzipan (almond paste). Allow to dry for a couple of days. Brush the marzipan with alcohol and coat with sugarpaste. Coat the board with the sugarpaste trimmings. Leave to dry for several days in a warm dry place.

● Cut a strip of paper the same depth as the cake. Measure the paper to fit one of the trifoil curves. Trace the template, see below, onto greaseproof paper (parchment) and scribe it on the cake side. Paint the bow and spruce, piping bulbs to represent the berries with red royal icing and a no. 0 piping tube (tip). Pipe a shell border around the cake, using a no. 2 piping tube (tip).

● Stamp out six Christmas trees with the cutter from thinly rolled pastillage and cut them in half, taking care not to distort them. Leave to dry on wax paper. Then dust them with blue or green lustre dusting powder (petal dust/blossom tint) and attach four half trees to each indent with royal icing.

● Trace the design, see page 66, onto greaseproof paper and scribe onto the sugar-paste coating, taking care that it is in line with the scallops of the cake. Paint the picture, following the step-by-step instructions on pages 36 – 37.

● Using a no. 0 piping tube (tip), pipe 40 lace pieces onto wax paper. When dry, remove the lace from the paper and attach to the cake with dots of royal icing to form a frame around the painted picture.

PAINTING RUNOUTS

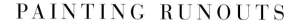

~ 1 ~

Runout the kitten motif in white royal icing, thinned to the right consistency with egg white. The ribbon, handle and point of the umbrella are runout in pink royal icing. Pipe royal icing around the edge of the umbrella to represent frills, using a no. 0 piping tube (tip).

*A guide to drawing
crimped pattern
and marking dots
on scallop section.
Adjust the pattern according to the cake size.*

EXPERT ADVICE

≈

It is always best to paint eyes in a lighter colour. If a mistake is made, it can be more easily rectified. Then outline in black to sharpen the features.

~ 4 ~

Paint the blue bird, taking care to keep the brush almost dry to prevent the moisture from dissolving the sugar of the runout. Paint blue eyes on the kitten and a yellow beak and feet on the bird.

~ 2 ~

Mix pink colouring with plenty of water or clear alcohol to make a pale tint. Remove the excess water from the brush with absorbent kitchen paper. Paint in highlighted areas and the nose. Trace on the eyes, taking care not to apply too much pressure as this could break the runout.

~ 3 ~

Outline the eyes with brown colouring. Use a fine brush and light blue and pink colouring to shade the umbrella.

~ 5 ~

Start to paint the fur on the kitten in the direction of the fur growth. Make short brush strokes about 5mm (¼ in) long. It will take time for the picture to become realistic so do not get disheartened!

~ 6 ~

Continue to paint the fur with darker shading by adding a little black. Paint the pupils, leaving a white dot in both eyes. Outline the ribbon, umbrella handle and point, eyes and eye lashes and bird's eyes, beak and feet with black. Paint the paving stones pink and blue.

RUNOUT CAT CAKE

25cm (10 in) round fruit cake
1.5kg (3 lb) marzipan (almond paste)
1.75kg (3½ lb) sugarpaste, coloured pink
250g (8 oz) royal icing
EQUIPMENT
33cm (13 in) round cake board
no. 0 and 1 piping tubes (tips)
no. 2 crimper
selection of food colourings
no. 0/4 and 2 paintbrushes
1m (1yd 3 in) x 3mm (⅛ in) red ribbon
1m (1yd 3 in) x 1cm (½ in) red ribbon
1.25m (1½ yd) x 1cm (½ in) silver paper
band for cake board edge

● Cover the cake with marzipan (almond paste) and coat with sugarpaste. Immediately after applying the sugarpaste, measure the circumference and depth of the cake and cut a strip of greaseproof paper (parchment) to these measurements. Fold this strip into eight sections and cut one edge into scallops. The lowest part of the scallops should come one-third of the way up the side of the cake.

● Attach the scalloped strip to the cake, using masking tape across the join to hold it in position. Starting at the centre of the scallop and working to each side, crimp the sugarpaste, keeping the amount of crimping on each scallop identical. Leave to dry.

● Cut one scallop section from the top of the side template. Draw the crimped pattern on the template. Using a ruler, mark dots radiating from each point of the crimping evenly, see page 40.

● Prick the dots onto each side section with a pin. Using a no. 1 piping tube (tip) and deep

pink royal icing, pipe the dots.

● Attach 1cm (½ in) ribbon to the bottom border and pipe a small snail's trail with a no. 1 piping tube (tip).

● Runout the kitten in white royal icing. Use pink royal icing for the ribbon around the kitten's neck and the handle and point of the umbrella. Leave to dry, then paint following the step-by-step instructions on pages 40 – 41.

● Cut out a 18cm (7 in) circle of thin card. Divide into equal sections. Use this template as a guide for the ribbon insertion. Offset the ribbon bow and attach with a small dot of royal icing. Pipe small dots in between the ribbon insertion using a no. 1 piping tube (tip). Remove the runout from the wax paper and attach to the centre of the cake with royal icing. Trim the board with silver cake band.

EXPERT ADVICE
≈

If you are not confident enough to paint directly on the coating, cut out a sugarpaste plaque and leave to dry. Paint the picture on the plaque.

Another advantage of using a plaque is that it can be removed from the cake and kept as a souvenir of the celebration.

Good quality brushes will always help to achieve good results in painting as they have a fine point, and keep their shape whilst painting. Sable are the best quality.

DECOUPAGE

Three-dimensional pictures, sometimes called decoupage, are an effective way to bring movement and life to designs. The idea is taken from craft work in which pictures are cut out from decorative wrapping paper or card, then they are assembled in layers and stuck down to form a slightly raised image. When applied to sugarcraft, the effect is to create a more prominent 3-D result.

The process of making your own designs is simple. Cut three circles of tracing paper large enough to cover the picture. On the first circle, trace the whole picture. On the second circle, trace (from the previous drawing) all the details which appear to stand out or the portions you want to be in relief. Finally, on the last circle trace the portions that will appear closest to you in the design.

Runouts or cutouts may be used to build up the image. It is important that the pieces are as thin as possible and flat for easy assembly and to achieve a delicate effect. Otherwise the result is ugly if the pieces are too thick as the sides distract attention from the overall design and the 3-D effect is totally lost.

~ 1 ~

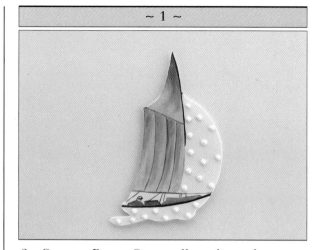

3D CUTOUT BOAT Cut cardboard templates, see page 70. Roll out the pastillage thinly. Cut out the pieces and leave to dry. On the first layer, paint only the details that can be seen when the boat is assembled. Pipe bulbs of royal icing on the back of the boat and attach it to the cake.

~ 1 ~

3D RUNOUT FISHERMAN Runout the designs, see page 70, in the appropriate colours. Paint the background. Attach first runout. Paint fishing line, back arm and paw. Use a no. 2 piping tube (tip) to pipe bulbs of royal icing over the runout which will be covered by the second layer.

~ 2 ~

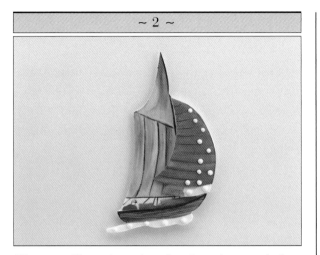

The pastillage is painted using the petal dust and fat method, see pages 10 – 11, as it is easier to achieve the shades on sails. Pipe bulbs of icing on the first layer, using a no. 2 piping tube (tip) and position the second layer. The icing helps to give extra depth to the picture.

~ 3 ~

Continue painting the pastillage pieces and assembling them on the picture with bulbs of royal icing. The background can be painted for extra detail. Trying to add more than three layers to a picture can spoil the effect and look untidy.

~ 2 ~

Paint the runout details, taking care not to spoil the gloss on the runout by having the brush too wet. If you do paint too much of the runout, it does not matter but there is no point if the hard work is to be covered by the next layer. Pipe bulbs of icing on the arm and nose.

~ 3 ~

Pipe scrolls of white royal icing around the figure to represent water. Attach the runout to the cake with bulbs of royal icing.

FISHING BEAR CAKE

*T*his cake would be ideal for a man's birthday or Father's Day. Adding keys or runout numbers would make a good design for a 21st or 18th birthday cake for a fishing enthusiast.

20cm (8 in) octagonal cake
apricot glaze
1.25kg (2½ lb) marzipan (almond paste)
clear alcohol (gin or vodka)
1.5kg (3 lb) sugarpaste
250g (8 oz) royal icing
selection of food colourings
EQUIPMENT
30cm (12 in) octagonal board (straight to straight)
greaseproof paper (parchment)
HB pencil
wax paper
no. 1 and 2 piping tubes (tips)
no. 0/4, 0 and 2 sable paintbrushes
1m (1 yd 3 in) x 5mm (¼ in) white ribbon to trim board
1m (1 yd 3 in) x 2.5mm (⅛ in) moss green ribbon to trim board

● Brush the cake with apricot glaze and cover with marzipan (almond paste). Brush the marzipan with alcohol and coat with sugarpaste. Coat the board separately with sugarpaste. Allow the coating to dry and secure the cake to the prepared board with a bulb of royal icing. If there is a small gap between the cake and board, use a no. 2 piping tube (tip) and royal icing to fill it, removing the surplus with a palette knife.

● Trace the templates for the side motifs, see below, and scribe on the cake. Paint with food colourings following the instructions on pages 40 – 41.

● Pipe three scallop rope borders around the base of each side, using a no.2 piping tube (tip) and royal icing. Overpipe each scallop with a drop loop of royal icing, using a no.1 piping tube (tip). Pipe three shells and a small bulb on each corner.

● Prepare the runout fishing bear on wax paper. Leave to dry, then paint the details following the step-by-step instructions on pages 40 – 41.

● Cut out an octagonal template 5cm (2 in) smaller than the top of the cake. Scribe a line on the coating round the template. Paint the background and position the run-outs. Pipe an 'S' scroll over the scribed line using a no. 1 piping tube (tip). Trim the board with the ribbons.

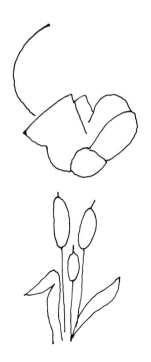

AIRBRUSHING

I find an airbrush with a small cup on the top to hold food colouring is the best. The types with bottles require a lot of food colouring and they are not so easy to clean out. If you do not have an airbrush, follow the same instructions for the background steps but use dusting powder (petal dust/blossom tint) and a 1.5cm (¾ in) chisel-ended brush. Always brush from the paper onto the cake. Stencils may be used for the diamond side motif, see pages 56 – 57. If you use orange and brown food colouring pens and paint in the diamonds, the result will be satisfactory.

MASKING CAKE TOP Cut a square of paper the same size as the top of the cake. Mark the paper 1cm (½ in) above the centre line on each side and tear the paper across this measurement. Cover the bottom portion of the cake with the torn paper.

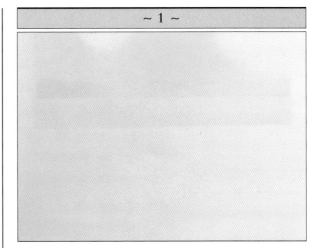

BASIC TECHNIQUE *Mask the cake top, see left. Place pieces of cotton wool in the left-hand corner and along the top for clouds. Airbrush light blue. Cover the blue part of the cake with paper and airbrush the green and gold strips.*

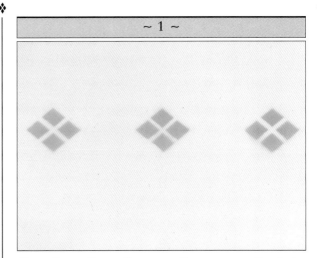

KEY CAKE SIDE STENCIL *Cut a stencil of the diamond shapes, see page 34, using a scalpel and oil board. Mask the surrounding area and exposed cake. Cover alternate diamond shapes with masking tape. Hold the stencil against the cake side and airbrush with orange colouring.*

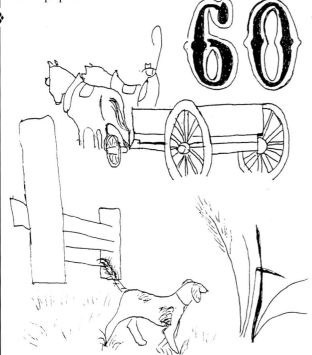

60th Birthday or Retirement Cake, see page 50

~ 2 ~

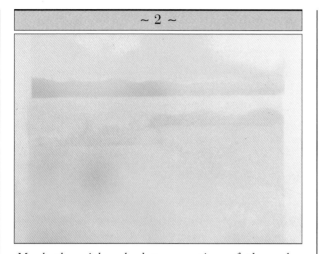

Mask the airbrushed top portion of the cake. Spray patches of blue in the centre and chestnut brown around the edge. It is always advisable to cover the sides of the cake and working area with paper to prevent colour accidentally being sprayed on them.

~ 3 ~

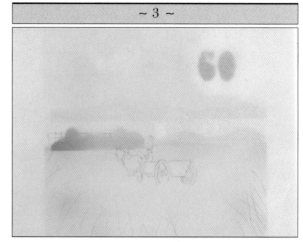

Make a stencil in oil board for the numbers. Use old gold colouring to spray through the stencil onto the corner of the cake. Trace the template of the horse and cart, see page 48, onto the dry airbrushed cake. Paint the picture using the direct painting method, see pages 36 – 37.

~ 2 ~

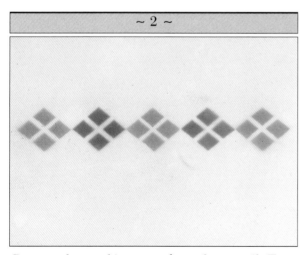

Remove the masking tape from the stencil. Tape over the diamonds between. Taking care to position the stencil accurately, airbrush with brown food colouring.

~ 3 ~

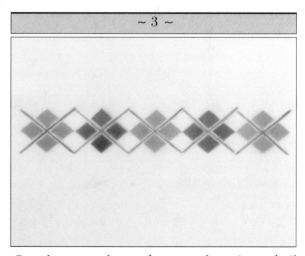

Cut the cross shapes from another piece of oil board. Airbrush the design, using alternate colours between the diamonds and taping as before.

60th BIRTHDAY OR RETIREMENT CAKE

18cm (7 in) square fruit cake
apricot glaze
875g (1¾ lb) marzipan (almond paste)
1.5kg (3 lb) royal icing
selection of liquid and paste food colourings

E Q U I P M E N T

18cm (7 in) square thin cake board
30cm (12 in) square cake board
airbrush ● wax paper for masking
oil board ● scalpel
HB pencil
greaseproof paper (parchment)
no. 0, 1, 2 and 4 piping tubes (tips)
ruler
no. 00, 0/4 and 2 paintbrushes
1.25m (1⅓ yd) brown ribbon to trim board

● Place the cake on the thin board. Brush the cake with apricot glaze and cover with marzipan (almond paste), then leave to dry for four days. Coat the cake and board with cream royal icing.

● When the royal icing is dry, airbrush the background, see pages 48 – 49, and paint the horse and cart, tree and grasses.

● Place wax paper over the collar design, see page 68, making sure there are no ripples in the wax paper. Outline the collar using a no. 1 piping tube (tip) and cream royal icing. Flood in the collar using softened icing. Pipe the scrolls on the collar with a no. 1 piping tube (tip) and leave to dry.

● Make a template for the board and outline in a tint of old gold royal icing, using a no. 2 piping tube (tip). Use the curves in the collar template to make a template for the side of the cake. Tilt the cake away from you and pipe the design using a no. 1 piping tube (tip).

● Secure the cake to the board with a small bulb of royal icing. Fill in any gaps in the bottom edge with icing before piping a bulb border using a no. 4 piping tube (tip).

● Carefully trace the design on the corner of the collar and paint the fence and dog, referring to painting on runouts, see pages 40 – 41. Remove the collar from the wax paper. Pipe a double line of royal icing, using a no. 2 piping tube (tip), around the top edge of the cake and position the collar. Pipe two lines inside the collar edge with no. 2 and 1 piping tubes (tips). Pipe brown dots with no. 1 piping tube (tip) on centre points of collar side and board design.

● Complete the cake by trimming the board with ribbon.

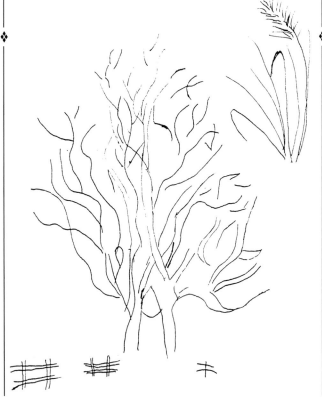

PUPPY CAKE

25 x 20cm (10 x 8 in) scalloped oval fruit cake
apricot glaze
1.25kg (2½ lb) marzipan (almond paste)
1.5kg (3 lb) sugarpaste
250g (8 oz) royal icing
clear alcohol (gin or vodka)
black food colouring
icing (confectioners') sugar
E Q U I P M E N T
38 x 33cm (15 x 13 in) scalloped oval board
greaseproof paper (parchment)
satay stick
scriber
straight frill cutter
no. 0 and 1 piping tubes (tips)
fine paintbrush
1m (1 yd 3 in) x 3mm (⅛ in) white ribbon
cocktail stick (toothpick)
HB pencil

● Place the cake on a large sheet of greaseproof paper (parchment). Brush the cake with apricot glaze and cover with marzipan (almond paste). Brush the marzipan with alcohol and coat with sugarpaste. Coat the board in sugarpaste. Immediately the board is coated, press a satay stick all around the edge of it, keeping the point towards the middle of the board. Leave to dry.

● Trace the templates for all the motifs, see also page 54, onto separate pieces of greaseproof paper. Turn the paper over and trace again. Turn the paper back to the original side. Scribe the motif on the centre of the cake and paint it following the step-by-step instructions, see page 54.

● Attach the cake to the board with a small bulb of icing. Roll out some sugarpaste thinly,

cut and make frills. Attach the frills to the board at the bottom edge of the cake, moistening the board with water or clear alcohol and fitting the straight edge of the frill to the bottom edge of the cake.

● Measure the depth of the side indent in the cake to where the ribbon is to end. Cut four pieces of ribbon to this measurement. Attach the ribbon with royal icing. Tie four ribbon bows and attach them to the ribbon on the top. Pipe embroidery on the cake top, using a no. 0 piping tube (tip). Pipe a small shell border with a no. 1 piping tube (tip).

~ 1 ~

Trace motif onto cake. When painting animals, use staggered lines to trace motif. Using a fine brush and black food colouring well mixed with water, start painting fur. Paint all solid lines. Use small strokes for the fur, following direction of growth. Then fill in body, keeping the brush quite dry.

~ 2 ~

Continue to build up fur, sometimes using undiluted colouring. The motif is built up using fine lines. Paint eyes quite dark, leaving white spots to give them a sparkle. Paint the mouse, mushrooms and foliage in the same manner. Stand back to see if any areas need darkening. Paint all side motifs.

STENCILLED CHRISTMAS CAKE

23 x 15cm (9 x 6 in) oblong cake
1.25kg (2½ lb) marzipan (almond paste)
1.25kg (2½ lb) sugarpaste
125g (4 oz) royal icing
black, red and green food colouring pens
small amount of pastillage
small amount of granulated sugar
EQUIPMENT
30 x 25cm (12 x 10 in) oblong cake board
manilla (oil) board
scalpel
no. 1 and 7 piping tubes (tips)
paintbrushes

● Cover the cake with marzipan (almond paste) and coat with sugarpaste. Place the cake on the board and allow the coating to dry before using a stencil.

● Make a stencil of the ribbon and holly, see page 69, for the side design. Outline the ribbon with a red food colouring pen and the holly with a green one. Paint the design with food colourings.

● Pipe shells from the cake to the board edge, using a no. 7 piping tube (tip). Cut a 'V' shape in a piping bag or use a leaf piping tube (tip). Fill the bag with green royal icing. Pipe a leaf and three red dots on each shell.

● Cut out the four balloon shapes, see below, in the pastillage, using the template. Allow to dry. Paint the balloons in red, yellow and green, leaving a white area on each to give the effect of the light reflection. Attach the balloons to each corner. Using a no. 1 piping tube (tip) and red royal icing, pipe the balloon strings.

● Make the stencil and following the step-by-step instructions, see pages 56 – 57, stencil the Father Christmas figure on the top of the cake.

● Paint holly and berries on each corner of the cake. Pipe the snow by Father Christmas's feet with white royal icing and sprinkle with granulated sugar to give a sparkling effect.

Illustrated on page 4

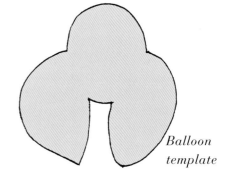

Balloon template

USING STENCILS

Stencils can be used in a variety of different ways. They can be purchased ready-cut, or copied from design books.

If you have an airbrush, you can spray through the stencil, covering the areas on which you want to use another colour with masking tape.

Stencilled lettering is easy to use and can produce some effective results. If, for example, old English lettering is required and you do not have time to make runout letters, stencils will provide the answer.

If you are using an old or professionally cut stencil, make sure it is clean before placing it on the cake.

Manilla (oil) board is available from art suppliers. It is very suitable for stencils as it is easily cut and water-resistant. Never immerse the board in water, just wipe it clean with a damp cloth.

EXPERT ADVICE

≈

The simpler and larger the shapes, the easier it will be to cut a stencil. The drawing should be clear and resemble a picture from a child's colouring book.

~ 1 ~

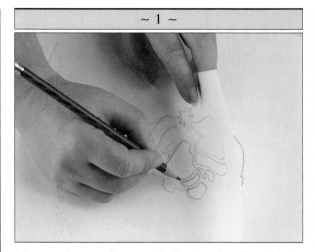

Trace the outline and basic details of the picture. Trace the picture again but this time draw each part on the inside edge, making each shape in the picture smaller.

~ 4 ~

Cut another stencil of just the fur, bobble and beard, see page 55. It is worth using a non-slip mat or cutting board when using a scalpel to prevent accidents.

~ 2 ~

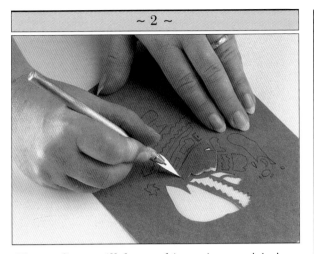

The outlines will leave thin strips, or 'ties' as they are known, to hold the stencil together. Trace the picture onto a piece of manilla (oil) board. Cut out the shapes using a scalpel, taking care not to cut through any of the 'ties'.

~ 3 ~

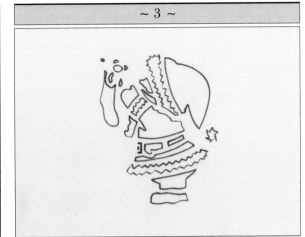

The stencil is now ready to use and once cut can be used many times. Place the stencil on the cake and outline with a black food colouring pen.

~ 5 ~

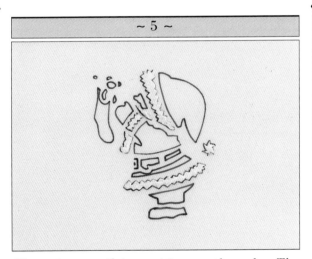

Place the stencil in position on the cake. The black outline below should be just visible. Spread white royal icing over the stencil with a knife and sprinkle granulated sugar over the icing. Carefully remove the stencil.

~ 6 ~

Mix red, black and peach dusting powders (petal dusts/blossom tints) with water on a palette and paint the Father Christmas figure. The result is quick but very effective.

~ 1 ~

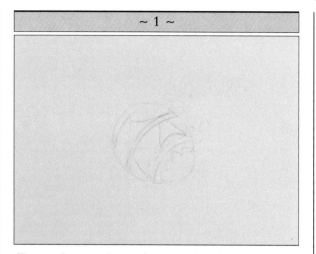

Trace the template of egg and viola design, see page 60, onto greaseproof paper (parchment). Retrace on the other side of the paper. Scribe the picture onto the cake. Do not trace grasses and foliage as it is difficult to keep to the lines when painting.

~ 2 ~

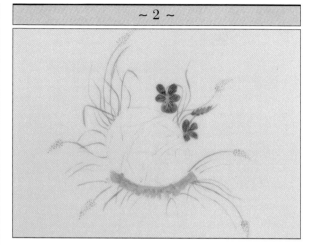

Using the direct painting technique, see pages 36 – 37, paint the violas and grasses. The violas shown here were painted with dusting powders (petal dusts/blossom tints).

~ 4 ~

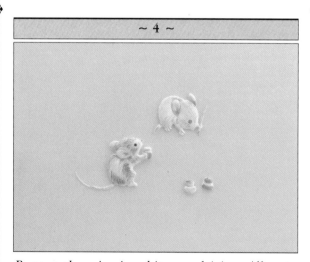

Runout the mice in white royal icing. Allow to dry. Following the instructions on page 37, paint the fur. Begin by painting the pink on the inside of the ears. Brush a selection of brown, black and cream in the direction of growth for the fur.

~ 5 ~

Position the mice overlapping the painted egg on the royal icing. Roll out the flower paste thinly. Using a scalpel, cut grasses. Use a ball tool on a cel pad or sponge to curve and twist some of them. Leave to dry for a few minutes only; they should be pliable.

~ 3 ~

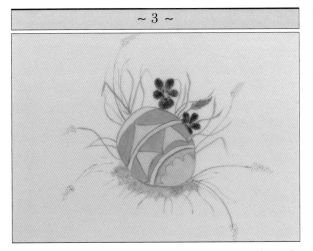

Paint the egg, using a no. 3 paintbrush, directly onto the cake. Outline the egg and violas in brown, using a fine brush.

~ 6 ~

Attach the sugar grass with egg white and violas with dots of icing. This cake illustrates how using a variety of techniques together can produce interesting designs.

EASTER CAKE

20 x 13cm (8 x 6 in) egg-shaped fruit cake
1kg (2 lb) marzipan (almond paste)
1kg (2 lb) royal icing
250g (8 oz) flower paste
selection of food colourings
victoria plum and lemon dusting powders (petal dusts/blossom tints)
3 sugar violas

EQUIPMENT

28 x 23cm (11 x 9 in) egg-shaped board
no. 0 and 1 piping tubes (tips)
greaseproof paper (parchment)
scriber
HB pencil
scalpel
selection of fine paintbrushes
ball tool
cel pad or sponge

● Attach the cake to the board. Cover with marzipan (almond paste) and leave to dry for several days.

● Colour 750g (1½ lb) of the royal icing a tint of melon with yellow food colouring. Set aside the remaining icing for the runouts and lace pieces. Coat the cake with royal icing.

● Prepare the runout mice, see left, in white royal icing. Pipe 60 viola lace pieces, using a no. 0 piping tube (tip) and melon-coloured royal icing. When dry, use victoria plum dusting powder (petal dust/blossom tint) on the top petals. Paint two black lines from the centre of the lace pieces, as indicated on page 60.

● Decorate the top of the cake, following the step-by-step instructions, left.

continued on page 60

continued from page 59

● Cut out a strip of greaseproof paper (parchment), the depth and circumference of the cake. Divide into four sections. Draw the scalloped design, making sure the pencil lines are all on the same side of greaseproof paper. With the pencil marks away from the cake, scribe the design onto the cake with the points of the scallops at the front, back and sides of the cake.

● Remove the template and scribe on the embroidery design. Pipe the embroidery with a no. 0 piping tube (tip) on the top and bottom borders with a scalloped piped design underneath the top border and above the bottom border with the same tube (tip). Attach the lace pieces to the cake on the scribed lines.

BABY GIRL'S BIRTHDAY CAKE

*T*his cake involves many of the skills already covered in step-by-step detail in this book. Cocoa and dusting powder painting is combined with 3-dimensional painted runouts and direct painting, together with sprays of sugar flowers.

28 x 20cm (11 x 8in) elongated hexagonal cake
1.5kg (3 lb) marzipan (almond paste)
1.75kg (3½ lb) sugarpaste
selection of food colourings
small amount of royal icing
cocoa powder and dusting powder (petal dust/blossom tint)
120 small cut-out sugar blossoms
3 sugar pansies
6 sugar daisies
EQUIPMENT
36 x 28cm (14 x 11 in) elongated hexagonal cake board
scriber
wax paper
1.5m (1⅔ yd) x 5mm (¼ in) ribbon to trim board
selection of paintbrushes

● Cover the cake with marzipan (almond paste) and coat with sugarpaste. Colour some sugarpaste yellow and cover the board. Attach the cake to the board with a small bulb of royal icing.
● Trace the templates for the toadstools and bunnies, see page 69. Scribe a toadstool on each corner of the cake and a bunny on each side. Using a mixture of cocoa and dusting powder, paint the designs, see pages 6 and 10.

● Pipe a shell border around the base of the cake, using a no. 1 piping tube (tip) and royal icing. Attach three cut-out blossoms to each angle of the cake board. Pipe sprays of shells to represent leaves.
● Scribe the flower design on the top of the cake. Paint the leaves and stems with food colouring, using a fine brush.
● Runout the 3D baby motifs, see page 69, onto wax paper. When dry, paint the features and details on the appropriate pieces. Assemble the picture with small bulbs of royal icing. Attach to the centre of the circle. The bubbles are bulbs of runout icing; when dry, colour with light blue shadows. Attach the flowers with small dots of icing. Complete the cake with ribbon around the board.

EXPERT ADVICE
≈

To secure ribbon or lace around a board, use a stick-type glue as this does not stain the ribbon. Make sure that the join is at the back. A small ribbon bow over the join gives a neat finish.

TEMPLATES

Christening Cake, page 8

Brush embroidery variations
(painting method), pages 18 – 19

Cocoa painting
(cricket design),
pages 6 – 7

Harvest Cake,
page 12

65

Strawberry Gâteau, page 22

Christmas Cake, page 38

Nanna Cake, page 16

Run-out Cat Cake, page 42

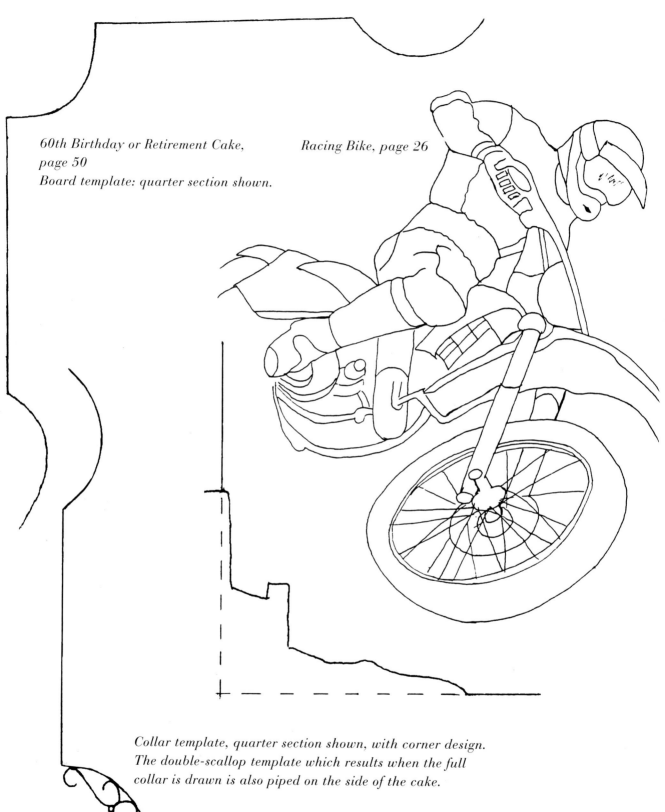

60th Birthday or Retirement Cake, page 50
Board template: quarter section shown.

Racing Bike, page 26

Collar template, quarter section shown, with corner design.
The double-scallop template which results when the full
collar is drawn is also piped on the side of the cake.

Baby Girl's Birthday Cake,
page 62

Stencilled Christmas Cake, page 55

3D Runout Fisherman, pages 44 – 45

3D Cutout Boat, page 44 – 45

Note: *These templates are reduced to 75 percent of the size required. Enlarge on a photocopier or by re-drawing using graph paper.*

Baby Girl's Birthday Cake, page 62

Brush embroidery, pages 14 – 15

INDEX

FOR FURTHER INFORMATION

Merehurst is the leading publisher of cake decorating books and has an excellent range of titles to suit cake decorators of all levels. Please send for a free catalogue, stating the title of this book:

United Kingdom
Marketing Department
Merehurst Ltd.
Ferry House
51 – 57 Lacy Road
London SW15 1PR
Tel: 081 780 1177
Fax: 081 780 1714

U.S.A./Canada
Foxwood International Ltd.
P.O. Box 267
145 Queen Street S.
Mississauga, Ontario
L5M 2B8 Canada
Tel: (1) 416 567 4800
Fax: (1) 416 567 4681

Australia
J.B. Fairfax Ltd.
80 McLachlan Avenue
Rushcutters Bay
NSW 2011
Tel: (61) 2 361 6366
Fax: (61) 2 360 6262

Other Territories
For further information contact:
International Sales Department at United Kingdom address.